A Match Made in Heaven

A Match Made in Heaven

A Bible-Based Guide to Deepening Your Relationship with God

NANCY REEVES

DIMENSIONS
FOR LIVING
NASHVILLE

A MATCH MADE IN HEAVEN
A BIBLE-BASED GUIDE TO DEEPENING
YOUR RELATIONSHIP WITH GOD

Copyright 2007 by Abingdon Press

All rights reserved.

This book is printed on acid-free paper.

Library of Congress Cataloging-in-Publication Data

Reeves, Nancy Christine, 1952-
   A match made in heaven : a Bible-based guide to deepening your relationship with God / Nancy C. Reeves.
      p. cm.
   ISBN-13: 978-0-687-64371-4 (pbk. : alk. paper)
   1. Spiritual life—Christianity.   2. Christian life.   3. Interpersonal relations—Religious aspects—Christianity.   I. Title.
   BV4501.3.R433 2007
   248.4—dc22

                                                              2006026763

07 08 09 10 11 12 13 14 15 16—10 9 8 7 6 5 4 3 2 1

In gratitude to Judi Morin,

who has accompanied many, including me,

on their quest to deepen their relationship with God

CONTENTS

ACKNOWLEDGMENTS

There are so many people who have helped in the writing of this book. I have space to name only a few here; the rest are held gratefuly in my heart. Thank you to

my psychological clients and spiritual directees for teaching me so much about God;

my husband, Bob Brinton, for his love and belief in the value of my writing;

my spiritual support system of Leslie and Henri, Linnea and David, Judi, and Anthony;

diana brecha for "hearing" the name for this book.

INTRODUCTION

Suggestions to help relationships flourish are made regularly on talk shows and in the latest self-help books. As a psychologist and spiritual director, I am particularly interested in assisting people develop healthy relationships with themselves, with others, and with God. So when I counsel others, I frequently use these psychological suggestions, which are usually based on an author's research or clinical experience.

One Sunday, however, I had an "aha" experience that radically changed me from focusing on the psychology of relationships to including the spirituality of relationships. I was listening as the pastor read from Proverbs 24. One particular verse drew my attention: "One who gives an honest answer gives a kiss on the lips" (v. 26). *Wow, what good psychology, I thought. A willingness to be honest truly is a loving act that deepens relationships.*

That proverb was good psychology as well as good spirituality. If quoted on a current talk show, most viewers would think it was a clever new insight. Yet this wisdom is thousands of years old. Long before the first psychological research on relationships was undertaken, our God spoke through the mouths of prophets to guide us in our lives. We can turn to the Holy Bible for psychological as well as spiritual wisdom! In fact, so much of modern psychological insight has roots in the word of God written thousands of years ago.

As I searched and found more psychology in scripture, I realized that the guidance was not solely concerned with our personal growth in faith or in developing healthy, intimate relationships with others. There is a great deal of guidance showing us how to deepen our relationship with God.

I believe that our God does not just want us to become "good" people, working for the kingdom of heaven as employees or servants. Jesus Christ told his followers, "I do not call you servants any longer, because the servant does not know what the master is doing; but I have called you friends, because I have made known to you everything that I have heard from my Father. You did not choose me but I chose you" (John 15:15-16). Much earlier, God spoke through the prophet Isaiah, saying, "You are precious in my sight, and honored, and I love you" (Isaiah 43:4). Scripture passages such as these point to an essential aspect of living as a Christian: deepening our relationship with our Triune God—Creator, Christ, and Holy Spirit.

I have chosen twelve scripture passages that speak to twelve principles intended to help us develop a deeper, richer relationship with our God. In the discussion of each of these principles, I have included stories from scripture as well as stories from my experience as a psychotherapist, spiritual director, and workshop and retreat guide. (The names and any identifying information of individuals mentioned have been changed.) I also have included findings from psychological studies. Although I have relied on scripture and psychology, the interpretations I have drawn are mine.

The main purpose of this book is to deepen our relationship with God. Many of the psychological principles refer to "loved one," and some of the examples I give are human-to-human ones. Yet always I suggest how to incorporate the concepts into the divine-human relationship. Even though our main focus is on our Divine Beloved, I hope that you will also find the book helpful for your human relationships. When relationships with the family members, friends, colleagues, acquaintances, and strangers in our lives are enhanced, that also has an influence on the divine-human relationship, for God wants us to love others. In the Gospel of Luke we read, "'You shall love the Lord your God with all your heart, and with all your soul, and with all your strength, and with all your mind; and your neighbor as yourself.' And he said to him, 'You have given the right answer; do this, and you will live'" (Luke 10:27-28).

Each chapter of the book includes the following elements:

- Psychological principle
- Scripture passage incorporating the principle
- Body of the chapter, with stories and concepts from scripture and psychology
- Relationship-building exercise, to do alone or in a small group

The end of the book contains a study guide to help readers use the material in a small-group setting.

Thank you for reading this book. I hope that it will help you on your spiritual path as you grow in faith, Christlikeness, and intimacy with God. May you know at your core that your relationship with God is truly a "match made in heaven."

Nancy Reeves

1

Say "I Love You" Frequently

*I love you, O L*ORD*, my strength.*
*The L*ORD *is my rock, my fortress,*
and my deliverer,
my God, my rock in whom I take refuge,
my shield, and the horn of my salvation, my stronghold.
(Psalm 18:1-2)

The term *love* is so much a part of today's culture that it has lost some of its power. "I loved that meal," "I love that television program," and similar statements are heard daily. And yet, the experience of being deeply in love is light years away from "I love your new carpet."

The fascination with every movement your new baby makes, the heart-melting embrace of old friends, and the earthshaking glance of young lovers evoke words such as *wonder, awe, adoration, reverence, tenderness, passion, ardor, intimacy, desire, attachment,* and *devotion.* This type of loving is done with our whole being. If we bring ourselves only partially to love, our beloved will immediately sense the lack.

Remember a time you were deeply in love. You likely experienced some of the following: wanting to be with the beloved at all times, thinking constantly about the loved one, wanting your beloved's highest good, becoming interested in the loved one's interests. You may have had physical sensations: rapid heart rate when thinking about or being in the presence of the one you loved; feeling light, as if you were "walking on air"; or feeling tingly or flushed. Often this type of love is accompanied by greater love for others or a feeling of being one with all creation. Deep love may result in times of "losing self" as your physical, mental, emotional, and spiritual boundaries disappear and you and your beloved are one.

Would you like this experience with God? God wants it with you. In fact, it is a frequently repeated theme in scripture: "Love the Lord your God with all your heart, and with all your soul, and with all your strength, and with all your mind; and your neighbor as yourself" (Luke 10:27).

Why would God put such an emphasis on love, rather than another quality? As it says in 1 John 4:16, "God is love." Since God's very essence is love, all life is made from, through, and with love. Divine power is the power of love. So, Love loves us and asks for our love in return.

The Benefits and Challenges of Love

A great deal of research shows that there is a positive connection between love and well-being. There are both physical and mental benefits to loving. Unfortunately, loving is not always easy. As a clinical psychologist, I find that the majority of concerns people bring me involve love. I hear about not enough love, too much (clinging) love, fear of love, the wrong type of love, the death of a love, or the death of love in an ongoing relationship.

Some of these love issues are also issues that people have in their relationship with God. They may believe that God loves everyone unconditionally—except themselves—or that they are special and God loves them more than others. Beliefs such as these keep some individuals from growing in their relationship with God. Other people realize these beliefs are untrue and long to move beyond these roadblocks in their relationship with God,

yet they don't know how. Still others may have a healthy understanding of God and God's love, yet they, too, long to grow in
their relationship with God. Although the twelve principles I
will be describing in this book are separate and distinct, they con-
tain a common theme: how to deepen our relationship with God.
Because no relationship can deepen without love, each of the
twelve principles illustrates an aspect of how to love God more
fully, as well as how to expand our capacity to accept the never-
ending, unconditional love of our Beloved.

Love and Fear

When it comes to accepting the love of our Beloved, one of
the most common hindrances is fear. One day Margaret came to
talk with me about her relationship with God:

> I've been reading some scripture every day, praying with it,
> and writing in my gratitude journal each evening. I thought
> I was doing all this to become a better Christian. Well, I'm
> changing in ways I haven't expected. Instead of just being
> kinder and more loving to others, things I associate with
> Christianity, I've been acting strange—kinda like I did when
> I was a teenager and met my first love.
>
> This feeling started when I was walking my dog in the
> woods, and the trees suddenly seemed so sacred. It was awe-
> some! My heart felt like it was expanding in my chest and I
> said out loud, "Oh, my God, what a wonderful world you
> have given me! Thank you." I stood for a long time gazing at
> God's gift to me, and my love for God grew and grew.
>
> When I returned home, my eight-year-old daughter said I
> looked like I was in love. I actually giggled in response! For
> the past week, I have been experiencing all the "symptoms"
> of falling in love. I see God's "gifts" to me everywhere—this
> wonderful world, my family and friends, my talents. I feel like

I'm floating, and the whole world has taken on a rosy glow. Every love song on the radio seems to be about me and God. Yesterday as I picked up my Bible, it fell open to the Song of Solomon, and I read, "My beloved speaks and says to me; Arise, my love, my fair one, and come away" (2:10). I'm sure I sat for twenty minutes feeling loved. God is wooing me!

After Margaret and I rejoiced together about her deepening relationship with God, she suddenly got a worried look on her face. "There's just one thing bothering me," she said. "When I'm feeling so much in love, I'm not afraid of God. My grandmother was always quoting scripture about the importance of 'the fear of the Lord.' And yet, I'm not afraid."

"Fear of the Lord" does appear numerous times in scripture. Yet as *Vine's Complete Expository Dictionary of Old and New Testament Words* explains, "the fear of the Lord" is a "wholesome dread" of displeasing God, rather than a fear of divine "power and righteous retribution."

Although this feeling of fear may arise, at times, in our relationship with God, it usually doesn't last long. Generally such a feeling is part of the experience of awe, which is a feeling of reverential respect mixed with fear or wonder (*New Oxford American Dictionary*).

Loving God fully—with our body, mind, heart, and spirit—encourages awe, with its mixture of fear and wonder. At times we will be touched with wonder; at times stabbed by fear. Yet this fear is not of what God will or will not do. It is fear brought on by the perceived threat to our "status quo," our existing state. The good news is that when we give ourselves in love, we change! We experience ourselves as new creations, refined and transformed by love.

Ironically, the flash of fear that comes with deep love and awe is psychologically and spiritually healthy. It helps us realize how precious God is to us, and it reminds us that God has relinquished power over us by giving us free will. We are loved so much that we have the freedom to accept or reject our Beloved's advances.

If, however, we hold on to our flash of fear, it becomes unhealthy. "Living in fear" is restrictive. We focus on our unworthiness to be in relationship with God and on the many wrongs we have committed. We expect God to act in threatening or punishing ways toward us. Our spiritual practices become directed toward placating a punitive Deity. The result is a lowered self-esteem, a wounded self-image, and a distorted image of our Creator.

Through scripture, through the action of the Holy Spirit in our lives, and in many other ways, we are urged to move closer to God, to understand more about our Love. As we experience God's reality, the distorted, hurtful images and beliefs about our Creator are transformed. Then, as we experience the fear of the Lord, it is an awe-filled wonder that benefits us, rather than a dysfunctional fear that restricts us. We are able to cherish the reality of our God.

Saying "I Love You"

How do you know someone loves you? If they just say the words without demonstrating their love, you probably won't believe them. Likewise, putting time and energy into your love for God is important. We can demonstrate our love for God in many ways, and the remainder of this book explores some of these ways.

I believe it is also important to say the words "I love you." A number of people have difficulty doing this because of the commitment saying those three little words implies. And yet, that is why we need to tell God of our love. Saying "I love you" lets God know that we are accepting this relationship of love and are committed to deepening it. So, let us say with the psalmist,

> I love you, O Lord, my strength.
> The Lord is my rock, my fortress, and my
>   deliverer,
>   my God, my rock in whom I take
>   refuge,
>   my shield, and the horn of my
>   salvation,
>   my stronghold. (Psalm 18:1-2)

Relationship-Building Exercise: Attributes of God

1. What do you love about God? Choose the seven divine attributes that touch you most deeply. You might choose attributes such as faithfulness, unconditional love, compassion, creativity, vulnerability, mercy, power, and tenderness. If it is challenging to come up with seven attributes right away, give the process some time. It may help to think of some of your favorite hymns or scriptures. What attributes do they demonstrate or describe?

2. After you have identified seven divine attributes, focus on a different attribute each day for one week. If compassion is the attribute of the day, for example, begin by giving thanks for how you have experienced God's compassion throughout your life. Ask God to help you remember some of these times of compassion. As you finish remembering, set your intention to become more aware of God's expression of compassion throughout the coming day. Then, live your day being sensitive to God's compassion manifesting itself through other people, the natural world, your inner experience, and so forth.

3. As you ready yourself for bed each night, remember with gratitude the flow of the day. Remember how you expressed your love for God throughour the day. Remember that simply doing this exercise is one way you expressed your love for God.

2

Say and Show Gratitude

I trust in the steadfast love of God forever and ever.
I will thank you forever,
because of what you have done. (Psalm 52:8b-9a)

My parents taught me that saying thank you was good manners. A civilized person is polite and expresses gratitude. I grew up thinking that gratitude was something I gave to others without receiving anything back. Now I realize that there are benefits for both receiver and giver.

Anna learned about gratitude after the death of her husband:

Even though other people were very caring and I knew God was sustaining me, I withdrew from everyone. I thought I was protecting my heart by holding back love and compassion. I was like a wounded animal hiding in the bush. Then, I sat down to send thank-you notes to everyone who helped me after Jim's death. I had to push myself to do it. I told myself that saying thank you was my duty as a Christian. As I wrote letter after letter, however, I began to feel held in invisible bonds of love, and I wasn't so alone anymore. My heart began to come out of hiding. I didn't realize being grateful would be so helpful even for my own healing.

Expressing Gratitude to God

There are thousands of hymns and prayers that say thank you to God. We often write, sing, and say them, not because it's the "right" or expected thing to do, but because we have a need—a deep desire—to express our gratitude to God.

Colin and Irene came to me with a desire to communicate more effectively in their marriage. One of my suggestions was to acknowledge appreciation for the other by showing gratitude. They agreed to practice; and the next time we met, the couple told me how beneficial that practice had been.

"I didn't realize what a treasure Colin is to me until I started thanking him," said Irene.

"And we haven't just been thanking each other," added Colin. "Last Sunday in church we sang one of my favorite hymns, 'How Great Thou Art.' What a wonderful song of gratitude to God! As I sang, I felt the gratitude burst out of my heart and expand through my whole body. After the service, Irene and I started listing all the things for which we are grateful to God."

Irene chuckled, and Colin stopped talking so she could add, "And we realized that we could never come to the end of our list! Every new moment is chock-full of God's grace. Every new moment gives us something else to be thankful for."

The couple and I discussed how showing gratitude helped them "see" the other more clearly, resulting in a closer connection. Gratitude deepens the bonds in relationship, whether the relationship is with another person or with our Beloved.

Saying thank you to God is just part of being grateful, however. We also need to act on our gratitude. One way is to acknowledge and use the gifts God has given us. I may be rich in creativity; but if I don't use it, what good is it to myself or others? Unfortunately, many people do not show gratitude for the gifts they have been given. They see them as unimportant or inferior to the gifts others have received.

The qualities and characteristics we were born with make up the unique persons we are. Each aspect of ourselves needs to be acknowledged, honored, and explored. Each will help us grow into the freedom God longs for us to have. Demeaning or dismissing part of ourselves has a negative effect on the whole.

The apostle Paul talked about the importance of honoring all our gifts, because each has an important place in the Body of Christ (1 Corinthians 12:1-7, 11). And we may not realize the value of each until we have acknowledged it and used it for awhile.

Some of the gifts God has given us are easily unwrapped and used. Others seem to come with a detailed instruction manual written in a foreign language. It is only by asking the Spirit's help that the gift can be "put together." To help us use our gifts effectively, sometimes the Spirit nudges us into a formal or informal education program. Other gifts may not be visible until we reach a certain age or experience a particular need. One woman said in amazement, "I never thought I had inner strength until I was out of a job after my company downsized. I didn't 'crumble' like I expected to. I have been able to draw on a vast store of inner strength I didn't know I had."

So, being grateful has two components: speaking and doing. For some people, however, both are difficult. Let's turn now to a common reason for this inability.

Overcoming Feelings of Unworthiness

Have you ever received a gift and responded, "Oh, you shouldn't have. I don't deserve it"? Or have you shown appreciation for something and heard in reply, "Oh, it's nothing"? Some people turn away praise to show that they are not conceited or filled with unhealthy pride. Others, however, really mean it when they say, "I'll never amount to anything," or "I don't deserve that."

The dictionary defines *unworthy* as "having little value or merit." If we actually believe that this describes us, our self-esteem and self-image will suffer. We will develop attitude and behavior patterns that diminish us—certainly not a grateful response to being created in God's image and likeness and being given authority over the rest of creation! And yet, some Christians believe they are to abase themselves before God. They concentrate on their sins—their failings—which doesn't leave them much time and energy to cherish and use their gifts.

Some people focus on their sins because they think God wants them to do so, yet this is not the message Jesus gave us. He taught that God is Love, and that God focuses on freeing us from our restrictions so that we can love more fully. Of course, bringing our wrongdoings to God is important, as we will discuss in a later chapter.

Another reason we may feel unworthy is that we have had an experience of God's awesome nature and, subsequently, feel insignificant compared to God's glory. One day Ruth said to me, "I'm not worthy of God's love." I told her that if any human had to be "worthy" of God, no one would qualify. Fortunately God is not looking for worthiness in us to decide whether or not to be in relationship. God committed to us prior to our birth. Jesus healed people without inquiring into their "worthiness" or asking if they would agree to stop sinning if he healed them. If we do not value ourselves as God's wonderful creation, acknowledging and being grateful for the many gifts our Creator has given us, our relationship with God will be adversely affected.

No loving parents want their children to cringe before them. Neither does our Loving Parent. If you find it difficult to let go of unworthy feelings that diminish you and your relationship with God, take the problem to prayer. Know that the Holy Spirit will guide you in ways to transform this hurtful pattern. You may receive insights that help you think differently, or encouragement to see yourself as God sees you, or a divine "nudge" to seek out appropriate books or a counselor. You may be drawn to scripture that shows you are "wonderfully made." You may also find the following relationship-building exercise helpful.

Let us rejoice and be grateful for God's ongoing gifts to us, knowing that we are beloved children. Let us give thanks by using our gifts to the best of our ability and in partnership with God. Let us not take God for granted, failing to appreciate the Divine Presence who is a constant in our lives. Instead, let us frequently express our gratitude that God desires a relationship with us, and say with the psalmist, "I trust in the steadfast love of God forever and ever. I will thank you forever, / because of what you have done" (Psalm 52:8b-9a).

Relationship-Building Exercise: Gifts

1. Choose one of the many gifts that God has given you. Move into prayer and thank God for this gift. Remember how it has changed or grown over the years.

2. Draw a timeline from your birth to the present. Write a word or phrase on your timeline about memorable incidents involving this gift that you recall. You may also wish to journal some of them in more detail. Give thanks.

3. Now focus on how you perceived God's presence in your use of this gift. How did God guide you, challenge you, support you, and so forth, to use your gift so that its impact on your life and the lives of others was more positive? Give thanks.

4. How do you experience this gift in your life right now? Set your intention for the manner in which you wish the gift to be manifested, with God's help, now and in the future. This may be general, such as "for my highest good," or more specific, such as, "I wish to give more time to . . ." Give thanks.

3

Give Care and Attention to the Relationship

But as for you, return to your God,
hold fast to love and justice,
and wait continually for your God. (Hosea 12:6)

 was speaking in a workshop about the need to give care and attention to our relationships. One woman disagreed. "I have a close friend I see only once every few years," she said. "When we get together, it's like we've never been apart." I asked if the contact with her friend had always been so sporadic. "Oh, no," she responded. "We met in sixth grade and were inseparable until I moved away to college. Then we arranged to work summers at the same restaurant so we could be together. But, for the past ten years, our meetings have been few and far between."

"So, your relationship started with a very firm foundation," I replied. "You had time to get to know each other, your likes and dislikes, your gifts and challenges, your joys and pains; and you built up a lot of shared history. That base allowed you to keep the close feeling when it was not possible to have frequent, direct contact."

"I hadn't thought of it like that," said the woman. "As you spoke, I was remembering that there were times of struggle and estrangement in the early years of our relationship. Working through those brought us closer together. That 'firm foundation' does give me a strong sense of trust and faith that we will always be close friends."

So it is with the divine-human relationship. It takes time to really get to know another—although an infinite God can never be fully known. Giving time, care, and attention to the relationship, though, bears much spiritual "fruit," all of which leads to a deeper relationship with our Beloved.

Relationship Builders

Christians throughout the ages who have wanted to develop a deeper relationship with God have realized the importance of daily spiritual practice. Spiritual practices such as prayer, meditation, singing, worship, and any other activity where we hold the conscious intention to be more receptive to God's presence in our lives are relationship builders.

No one spiritual practice is "better" or "holier" than another. I believe God invites us to the practices that will help us in the particular way that we need at that moment in our lives. Brandon related how praying with scripture was a daily practice of his for many years. Then he became aware in prayer of a repeated urge to walk. After a time of resisting the urge, and then a time of experimenting with various ways of responding to it, Brandon found a new daily practice. Currently he does a walking meditation each morning, and he has found his image of God and experience of divine presence greatly expanded. Scripture is still important to him, although he realized he was limiting God and himself by solely focusing on the written word.

Think of a close friend. I imagine you do more than one kind of activity with this person. What you do together may depend on your needs, interests, time of day, time of year, or time of life. Similarly, if we know a variety of spiritual practices, we can be more easily guided by the Holy Spirit to the one activity that will deepen our divine-human relationship most effectively right now. Some practices are for daily use, such as giving thanks prior to eating, making time for prayer or meditation, reading and reflecting on Scripture, or writing in a journal. Other practices are for specific or infrequent use, such as healing services, group worship, or programs at retreat centers and church camps. Still other practices are associated with various times in the church year.

The plethora of spiritual practices can be overwhelming. And some people take every new course and try every new type of prayer they come across. Care and attention to the divine-human relationship, though, has more to do with quality than quantity. It includes taking time to become familiar with the spiritual practices we are guided to by God. The Bible describes Jesus' own spiritual practices as well as two practices he taught his disciples.

Two Spiritual Practices Taught by Jesus

Christ gave his relationship with God much care and attention, so it is no surprise that daily spiritual practices were important to him. There are numerous examples in scripture of Jesus praying alone; praying in community; praying prior to healing another, as well as when he needed healing himself; and giving thanks to God before every meal.

The first practice Jesus taught us is the prayer called the "Our Father" or "The Lord's Prayer." There are two slightly different versions of this prayer in Matthew 6:9-13 and Luke 11:2-4. Whichever version you read, it is clear that this short prayer is full of relationship issues. The first words Jesus says, "Our Father," indicate our relationship to God. We are children, not subjects. In fact, the word Jesus used for Father meant "daddy," an approachable, beloved parent. The rest of the prayer speaks of a number of different aspects of relationship. I believe this prayer deserves our care and attention. Saying it slowly, pausing to ask "What does this mean to me right now?" after each line, may give us insights into how God wishes us to walk our Christian path at this moment in time.

Another spiritual practice initiated by Jesus became a core experience for the Christian church. We read about it in Luke 22:14-20. It was the night before Jesus' crucifixion and one of the holiest feasts of the Jewish year, the Passover. Jesus and his disciples gathered together to share the feast. It was during this meal that Jesus initiated the practice that brings us into physical and spiritual fellowship with all other followers of Jesus as we take and share bread and wine. This spiritual practice is called by various names: the Eucharist (from the Greek for "thanksgiving"), Holy Communion, and the Lord's Supper. Christians vary in their beliefs about this practice. Some assert that the bread and wine are transubstantiated or converted into the actual body and blood of Christ. Others believe that this practice is a sacred memorial, a thanksgiving for God's presence in our lives, and a deeper opening to God's grace.

Whatever your beliefs, the Eucharist is a spiritual practice given to us by Emmanuel, God with us, hours before he was crucified. The bread and wine are potent reminders of the sacrifice Christ made because of his love for us.

Don't Take God for Granted

The divine-human relationship has been "granted" to us by our Beloved. However, if we "take it for granted"—if we fail to appreciate our connection because it is free and eternal—we show disrespect to the Giver, and we remain in the shallows of relationship. The prophet Hosea encourages us to give our relationship with God the care and attention it deserves: "But as for you, return to your God, / hold fast to love and justice, / and wait continually for your God" (Hosea 12:6).

We have discussed a number of benefits for and ways to give care and attention to our Beloved. I suggest you keep this relationship principle in mind as you read the other chapters, for every other principle in this book—such as love, gratitude, and forgiveness—will benefit from our increased care and attention. And that will deepen our relationship with our God.

Relationship-Building Exercise: The Church Year

This exercise is intended to help you open your mind and heart to the events of Jesus' life that the Christian church commemorates and celebrates throughout the calendar year. Find a list of events that make up the Christian year. (Good lists can be found in books and on the Internet.) Taking each event in turn, structure your thoughts and feelings by asking yourself questions 1-2. Question 3 is a general question.

1. What are some words or phrases that you associate with this time? (e.g., "birthing" at Christmas, "the gift of the Holy Spirit" at Pentecost)

2. Remember one or more experiences during this time that have deepened your relationship with God. Writing the experience may help you to include more details. If you do not have an experience from a particular holy day or season, move on to the next one on the list.

3. How can you be sensitive to the Christian year as you live through the calendar year?

4

Develop Self-Awareness
to Help the Relationship

To get wisdom is to love oneself; to keep understanding is to prosper. (Proverbs 19:8)

She approached when I was signing books at a conference. "I've been in five bad relationships, and each time I prayed to God for help in choosing the right partner. Obviously, God isn't listening; how do I get the Holy One's attention?"

I replied, "Do you have any sense of where your relationships went wrong?"

"Oh, yes," she responded. "It was all their fault. They couldn't make a commitment or were just too immature."

"Are you aware of some of the ways you, yourself, have difficulty being in relationship?"

"Oh, no, I told you, it was their fault, not mine. I have no problem being in a relationship. All I want is to get God to direct me to the right partner."

The young woman left abruptly when I said that no one is all good or all bad, and that awareness of personal challenges as well as gifts could only benefit our relationships. If she kept to her black and white stance, prognosis for future human partnerships did not look good. Her desire to find ways to "force God's hand" would not help her divine-human relationship either.

The proverb says, "To keep understanding is to prosper" (Proverbs 19:8b). Self-understanding or awareness helps us grow into the people we are meant to be. Without a willingness to grow in self-awareness, we are more likely to blame God for the ways we restrict ourselves. Blaming God for our misfortunes blinds us to the reality of our Creator and to our own reality. If we do not become aware of our own reality, which includes our restricting patterns as well as our gifts, we will act toward God the way that the young woman did in her human relationships—by judging and turning away.

True Self-Love

The writer of the proverb begins, "To get wisdom is to love oneself" (Proverbs 19:8a), and on the surface it appeared that the young woman I mentioned loved herself. Yet what she loved was a false image since she saw only her strengths. True self-love is not about being self-centered. It is about seeing our reality and loving this self that is made in God's likeness. Seeing our reality involves an intentional commitment to self-awareness, to developing an understanding of the unique human being each of us is. The goal of self-awareness is not to try to become perfect people but to cherish our gifts and be free of slavishly following restrictive attitude and behavior patterns.

So, how do we grow in self-awareness? How do we change the thoughts and actions that bind us? An important step is recognizing that the true change agent is the Holy Spirit, who is always encouraging, challenging, and guiding us in the way that leads to freedom. Whether we realize it or not, the process of transformation is a partnership between ourselves and God. We may find ourselves guided to self-awareness through reading books on psychology or spirituality, journaling, taking workshops, entering counseling, or seeking spiritual direction. The self-awareness we gain often leads to our intentional commitment to allow the Spirit to change us—to modify restrictive attitudes and behaviors.

Then, as we continue to learn, change, and grow, we become freer, more loving people.

I often refer to the attitudes and behaviors that restrict us as our "weeds." In Jesus' parable of the weeds, found in Matthew 13, Jesus is telling us that the kingdom of God is like a field where wheat and weeds grow together, and it is not our place to rip out all the weeds because that would damage the wheat as well. God will deal with these weeds later. As with all Jesus' teachings, this parable contains truth on many different levels., but I'd like to suggest a psychological interpretation. When we look around our world and within our ownselves, we see many "weeds"—war, injustice, selfishness, and so forth. I believe we can do something about some of these weeds—such as weaknesses, restrictive behavior patterns, and injustices—as we work in partnership with the Holy Spirit. I also believe there are other weeds that we can't get rid of; and if we put a lot of energy into trying, we won't have as much energy for growth.

The apostle Paul discovered something within him that was restrictive and called it his "thorn" (see 2 Corinthians 12:8-10). For a reason known only to God, Paul's thorn or weed needed to remain. Yet the Spirit helped Paul to find a meaning in his weakness that would strengthen his faith and deepen the divine-human relationship.

So, how do we know which weeds to tackle and which to leave alone? Ultimately, it is the Spirit who guides us in this. Growing self-awareness helps us to do our part by letting us see our weaknesses more clearly and realizing their effect on our relationship with God and our relationships with others.

The Ego

One aspect of ourselves that some people view as a huge weed is called our ego. As I worked with Janis on her desire to become more assertive, I realized she had quite a low self-esteem. When

I mentioned this to her, she responded, "Oh, I guess that's just me. I've always been like that." As she grew in self-awareness, however, she revised that earlier statement. "A low self-esteem isn't 'just me'; it's an attitude pattern I learned over many years," she acknowledged, "and it's starting to change." Janis was becoming more aware of messages her ego had given her, messages that originated in her relationship with her father. As our sessions progressed, she could start to see her own reality.

The ego is what we often think of as our conscious self. Our ego, in itself, is neither good nor bad. It helps us to learn who we are as we progress through the various stages of human development on our way to becoming mature adults. It is important to have a strong ego for healthy development.

Unfortunately, it is common for parts of our ego to be wounded by life experiences. Because our ego doesn't always discriminate well, it tends to believe without question the messages of those who have power and authority in our lives. The six-year-old hears, "You'll never amount to much," and takes it as truth. Even when reality shows a different picture, the child—and later the adult—is unable to see himself or herself as competent in life. Similarly, even though Janis had heard all of her life that God loved her unconditionally, she couldn't let herself believe it until she had developed some self-awareness.

So, getting to know our ego and identifying the messages it tends to give us makes it possible to realize when our ego gets off track. Then we won't automatically do what it says but will be aware when it is speaking out of its woundedness.

The Importance of Self-Awareness

Self-awareness helps us to deepen our relationship with God by showing us our "wheat" and "weeds." Some of the weeds will be transformed. Some will remain, and if we are aware of them, they will not be as restrictive. For example, if I am unaware of my tendency to try to make others feel guilty when I feel wronged, I will frequently act in this hurtful way. Once I have the realization, although I still will get the urge to make others feel guilty, I will be able to suppress that urge as I draw upon the power of the Holy Spirit within me.

Even if I do a lot of work to change this behavior, the tendency or desire to make others feel guilty may remain within me for my whole life, such as Paul's thorn. This will not hold me back from growing into deeper relationship with God, however, for living the Christian life means increasingly allowing the Spirit to express the life of Christ through us, moment by moment. Even though we know our restrictions, we also know that God's power working within us "is able to accomplish abundantly far more than all we can ask or imagine" (Ephesians 3:20).

Awareness of a weakness, then, helps by showing us, specifically, where to partner with the Spirit for healing and growth. Obsessing about our many sins and weaknesses, however, will not help us to grow or to deepen the divine-human relationship. Self-awareness shows us the wonderful "wheat" with which God has gifted us—the qualities that help us to be freer, more loving people. As we become more aware of these qualities, we can bring them more frequently and fully to all that we do, including our relationship with our Beloved. And as we acknowledge and work with both our wheat and our weeds, we can truly experience the truth of the proverb: "To get wisdom is to love oneself; / to keep understanding is to prosper" (19:8).

Relationship-Building Exercise: Seven Personal Qualities

1. As human beings, we have a combination of personal qualities that are unique to us. We view some of these qualities as helping us to grow, and some we judge as restricting who we are meant to be. Write down the seven qualities (whether you

consider them to be positive or negative) that you believe are most present in you. You might list qualities such as creativity, stubbornness, caring, perfectionism, and so forth.

2. Once you have listed your qualities, answer the following questions:

- How has each quality deepened my relationship with God?
- How has each quality hindered my relationship with God?

3. Give thanks to God for these qualities that make you the unique person you are.

5

Tell Your Loved One
What You Need

*"Ask, and it will be given you; search, and you will find;
knock, and the door will be opened for you. For everyone who
asks receives, and everyone who searches finds, and for everyone who knocks, the door will be opened." (Matthew 7:7-8)*

Why did Jesus tell us to ask, search, and knock? Surely an omniscient Creator already knows our needs and chooses whether or not to meet them. I believe that Jesus, in these words, was giving us good psychological and spiritual guidance. Let's examine some reasons why the practice of asking for what we need deepens our relationship with God.

Why Does God Want Us to Ask?

Over the years, many people who have come to me for coun-seling have been absolutely certain about their needs. I've heard the following statements hundreds of times: "In order to be happy, I need a better job ... more money ... my kids to respect me ... my boss to rely on me more." And yet, if their stated needs had been fulfilled, most of them would have found that they weren't as happy as they had expected to be.

C. S. Lewis says that we have a strong longing that starts in childhood, which we can easily misunderstand. For example, if we are thinking about a foreign country when we feel the longing,

39

we may believe we will satisfy it by traveling. Lewis says that we are truly longing for God, and that it may take many years of running after mistaken needs before we come to this realization. Augustine of Hippo in the fifth century said, "You have made us for yourself, and our heart is restless till it finds its rest in you."

When we ask God for what we think we need, our attention is directed toward our Creator. When God has our attention, it is easier for us to recognize our real need, which is a deeper divine-human relationship. Jesus said to his disciples, "My food is to do the will of him who sent me and to complete his work" (John 4:34). As Jesus implied, the "food" that truly sustains us is to do God's will.

So our deepest need is the same as what God wills for us. If we just follow God's will, our needs will be taken care of. Sounds simple, right? And it is. However, simple is not always the same as easy. For God's voice is not the only voice that tells us what we "should" want.

Ad agencies have recognized the growing interest in spirituality and intentionally play on this interest as they attempt to sell us their particular line of material goods. Likewise, the words of influential people in our past—even if they are no longer living—continue to speak within us. Friends, family members, church, society, and our own egos all think they know what is in our best interest. In fact, these voices are frequently "louder" than the often still, small voice of the Holy Spirit.

Because these other voices can be very subtle and persuasive, we must be intentional in talking with God about all our needs. Sometimes it can be difficult to know the first thing about our needs, especially when we are confused. So we must make it a practice to ask God to help us understand our needs.

There are a number of concepts and methods that will help us understand and follow divine will more closely. This process is called spiritual discernment, and it is the focus of chapter 6. At this point, let's look at one major stumbling block to understanding our deepest needs.

Unhealthy Attachments

It can be particularly hard to hear the Spirit's guidance in uncovering our deepest needs, and thus God's will, when we are attached to or invested in a relationship or object in an unhealthy way. Do you know of a relationship in which one person won't give the other freedom to change, or one in which one member decides what the other needs, or one in which a person seems completely dependent on another? These are examples of relationships psychologists call unhealthy attachments. A person who is too controlling or dependent, or who has some other type of unhealthy attachment, usually has low self-esteem. We also can have an unhealthy attachment to something other than a person. For example, we might give too much time or importance to our work, our possessions, our lifestyle, or even our bodies and mental faculties. Unhealthy attachments can range from mildly irritating to deeply hurtful.

There may also be times when we have an unhealthy attachment in our relationship with God. Then, we may be too dependent on our Creator, wanting God to fix our problems, rather than using the gifts we have been given. Or we may try to control God, demanding that the Holy One resolve our problems in the way we specify. Frannie told me, "It's embarrassing to admit, but I told God I wouldn't go to church or pray until I got the job I wanted."

Other unhealthy attachments include feeling envious or jealous of another's relationship with our Beloved, being angry at God for giving another the type of spiritual experience we long for, and believing that we must jump through spiritual "hoops" to earn God's love.

Each day, we need many things in order to live and to make life more satisfying. These needs range from food and shelter to love and acceptance. When we have unhealthy attachments in our lives, we believe that "more is better." We believe that "the end justifies the means." We begin to believe that we need much more than we really do. We take more than our fair share of the world's resources and think it is our right. Some people actually view their abundance as confirmation that they are especially favored by God. Learning to recognize unhealthy attachments within ourselves is important to developing a healthy, intimate relationship with God.

Healthy Attachments

It is clear that God's plan, God's desire for our lives, is that we have healthy relationships—with one another and with God. What are the qualities of a relationship with healthy attachments? "Love, joy, peace, patience, kindness, generosity, faithfulness, gentleness, and self-control" make up a list that could be found in numerous psychology books. This list, though, does not come from a psychological source. It was written about two thousand years ago by Paul of Tarsus in a letter to the members of a young Christian community (Galatians 5:22). The list describes the "fruit" or results of living in relationship with the Holy Spirit. This fruit, as with all gifts of God, is meant to be shared. Living these qualities in relationship with God and with other people encourages healthy attachments.

Another quality that promotes healthy attachments is respect. Respect, or having a deep admiration for another, is an aspect of healthy love. True respect implies desiring the highest good for another. If loved ones ask us for something that would diminish them, we do not show respect to acquiesce or meet that need because we know it's not in their best interest. Likewise, God, out

42

of love and respect for us, may not give us everything for which we ask. What we will be given is what we *really* need, although it may take years for us to realize this truth.

Jesus counseled us to change our priorities so that, instead of being self-centered, we become God-centered. He said, "Do not store up for yourselves treasures on earth, where moth and rust consume and where thieves break in and steal; but store up for yourselves treasures in heaven, where neither moth nor rust consumes and where thieves do not break in and steal. For where your treasure is, there your heart will be also" (Matthew 6:19-21). When our heart is in God, we have healthy attachments.

How do we know when our attachments are healthy? For me, my hands are a great indicator of how much I'm clinging to a particular person, idea, or object. When I really want a certain thing, I find my hands clenching into fists. When the attachment is healthy, my hands stay relaxed as I explore the various options or consider a certain purchase or other decision. Other people may become aware of other kinds of physical signals.

The relationship-building exercise at the end of this chapter invites you to explore healthy and unhealthy attachments in your own life.

Bringing Our Needs to God

Our Beloved always responds to our deepest needs, giving us the love, compassion, strength, and guidance that will help to meet those needs. If we are invested in having our needs met in a certain way, we may not see how God is actually fulfilling them. When we are open to the Spirit's movement in our lives, we may be surprised at how our needs are met.

There was a time in Jesus' own life when he asked God for one thing but was given something else—something that he truly needed. This experience occurred while he was in agony of heart and spirit the night before his crucifixion. Jesus prayed as he knelt on the Mount of Olives, "Father, if you are willing, remove this cup from me; yet, not my will but yours be done" (Luke 22:42). Trusting that God would respond to his asking, searching, and knocking, Jesus poured out his pain and concern in prayer. And we read in verse 43 that God met his deepest need, sending an angel to give Jesus strength to carry him through the subsequent arrest, beatings, farce of a trial, and horrific death. If Jesus had looked only for "the cup" to be removed from him, he might not have been receptive to the angel's gift of strength.

May we, like Jesus, with trust and love, bring our needs to God in prayer and thereby deepen our relationship with God.

Relationship-Building Exercise: Exploring Attachments

1. Remember a time when you were attached to something in an unhealthy way. Think or write about the situation.

2. Where and how do you "experience" or respond in your body to unhealthy attachments? Some examples might include clenched fists, a tight gut, and pressure in the head.

3. Remember a time when you were spiritually detached. Think or write about the situation.

4. Where and how do you "experience" or respond in your body to healthy attachments? Some examples might be a feeling of lightness in the chest, a warm softness in the stomach, and open, relaxed hands.

5. Move into prayer and tell God of your desire to live in the freedom of healthy attachments. Thank your Creator for the help you have already received with this, and for the guidance you are receiving now and in the future.

6

Consult with Each Other
When Making Decisions

*Just as the branch cannot bear fruit by itself unless it abides in
the vine, neither can you unless you abide in me. I am the
vine, you are the branches. Those who abide in me and I in
them bear much fruit. (John 15:4-5)*

Every moment of the day we are making decisions. Even
refusing to choose is a choice.

Because God desires that each of us receives the healing and
growth we need to reach our full potential, our Creator has
given us many gifts—qualities such as patience, trust, love, and
compassion; and talents such as intelligence, creativity, and prac-
ticality—as well as the guidance of the Bible and the indwelling
presence of the Holy Spirit to help us with our daily decisions.

When we consciously seek divine guidance, we are practicing
"spiritual discernment." Spiritual discernment is different from
"decision making," which I define as a process we employ to
come to a conclusion using our own resources. Spiritual discernment implies a conscious partnering with God that invites a
deepening of the divine-human relationship.

How God Guides

Spiritual discernment is more of an attitude than a method. The
attitude of discernment says, "I will be open for the often still, small
voice of the Spirit every day, in all that I do." Because God
is respectful of our free will, however, we often will not be told

outright what to do. Instead, we will become more aware of the nudges, the feelings of deep peace or rightness, the words of wisdom spoken by others, the books that seem to call to us from the library shelf, the seeming coincidences or synchronicities, the dreams, and the many other ways that God uses to get our attention.

Sometimes individuals are intentional in seeking guidance through a spiritual discernment method, such as contemplative prayer, that opens them to God's will. Frequently, however, God's guidance comes without the use of a discernment method—sometimes before we even know that a decision needs to be made!

There are times when our Beloved speaks guidance through our gifts, talents, and strengths. For example, Sandra has a gift for listening to people, which is one reason she is such a popular high school teacher. She realized some years ago that she often receives God's messages through "unintentional prophets" she meets on the bus riding to work. Sandra strikes up many conversations with strangers and often is given advice. In most cases, she knows the suggestions are of human origin.

Every so often, however, Sandra hears words that seem to "tingle" within her. She explains, "When this happens, I know that person is being a vessel for the Spirit. They usually don't realize this, although once an older man paused and said, 'That didn't come from me. Do you believe in God?' When I told him I did, he continued, 'Well, I don't know what those words meant for you, but I do know we've both just been blessed with the Spirit's presence.' We smiled at each other and sat in grateful silence until my stop came."

Sometimes it is not possible for us to hear God in a familiar way anymore. So, when our needs and abilities change, God may modify how guidance is sent. Eric had always heard God "speak" to him through Scripture. In the last few years, Eric had had a series of strokes, and, when I talked with him, his mind was very confused.

Eric told me he couldn't understand what he read anymore. After a period of frustration and depression as he tried to get meaning out of the written word, Eric gave up. Then he started to "hear" words of love, support, guidance, and encouragement in his mind. Eric said this was a very new experience for him, and he just knew he was being visited by angelic beings. The nursing staff at his retirement home told me his mood abruptly changed after the first "visit." His frustration and depression lifted. Now Eric often sits, beaming at everyone.

The stories of Sandra and Eric are just two examples of the many ways God may reach out to us in guidance. Developing an attitude of discernment helps us to recognize these ways in our daily life.

God's Refining Guidance

At times God sends us messages in an unfamiliar way in order to help us become freer, more loving people—in other words, to refine us.

Brent told me he valued his intellect and discredited his heart until he realized that God seemed to "speak" to him only through feelings. He knew God's will when he had a deep feeling of love or peace or enthusiasm. He explained, "I'm not an emotional person. I've always prized a calm, rational state of being. Whenever I asked God for guidance, though, it seemed to come from my heart instead of my head. I began to see how I was putting down an important part of me. It was a wake-up call for me, challenging me to be the person God knew I could be."

The story of Samuel and Eli found in 1 Samuel 3 is an example of another of God's "wake-up calls." Although this story may appear to be only about a divine message for the young boy, Samuel, it also has a very strong message for the old priest, Eli. A little earlier in First Samuel, we read about Eli's sons: "Now the sons of Eli were scoundrels; they had no regard for the LORD or for the duties of the priests to the people" (1 Samuel 2:12). Eli heard about the wrongdoing of his sons and confronted them, but they would not change their ways. For whatever reasons, Eli did nothing further to stop them. So the Eternal One sent a messenger to Eli, a man of God, who told Eli that there would be terrible consequences for himself and his family if his sons did not stop their hurtful behaviors. Eli still did nothing.

Then, God called to Samuel three times, and the boy went to Eli. By the third time, Eli realized God was talking to Samuel, and he instructed Samuel how to answer. Although he ignored it, this was another message for Eli. The fact that God spoke to the young child instead of to the priest shows that the consequences of the sons' misdemeanors had already begun.

There was yet another message. When God called Samuel for a fourth time, the boy responded and was told of the ruin that would occur in Eli's family. The next morning, Eli asked what God had told Samuel, and the message was reported to him. After listening, Eli acknowledged to Samuel, "It is the LORD," but still he did nothing to stop his sons.

When we get "off track," when we do not follow God's commandments, when we act in life-restricting ways, God responds. The Holy One does not respond with punishment but with loving guidance. Repeatedly and with varying methods our God invites us to return to having right relationships, to walking in God's ways. The story of Samuel and Eli is a wonderful example of how God's guidance is intended for the highest good of all. Samuel realized that God wanted a personal relationship with him; Eli was reminded of the consequences of his inaction. If Eli had only asked God's help to curb his sons, that assistance would have come.

The stories of Brent and Eli demonstrate the "tough love" guidance of the Holy Spirit. Brent said yes to God's guidance and grew; Eli said no and suffered the natural consequences of acting in ways that were harmful to himself and others. God's will is that we turn away from attitude and behavior patterns that harm or otherwise diminish us. It is our choice, though, whether or not we heed that guidance.

In any case, following God's will often can be difficult, especially when God asks us to do things we don't want to do. We must remember that because God's very essence is Love, our Creator always calls with and through love. If we think we are being called to do something that will diminish us, we must remember to question our Beloved. Due to many factors such as fatigue, poor self-esteem, ignorance, and unfamiliarity with divine-human interactions, we sometimes can get the message wrong. If we ask God questions about the when, how, and where of something, an answer may come that suggests, "Wait, and you'll know," or "Ask your friend," or "Listen when you're with your family."

Asking and waiting patiently for further guidance may help, although we can't expect God to give detailed answers to all our queries. Some discerners find it helpful to take a step or two down the path and then examine their progress to see if their actions are "building the kingdom" by producing spiritual fruits, such as increased love, compassion, justice, and kindness.

Deepening Our Relationship with God Through Spiritual Discernment

There is no room in this chapter to adequately explore even a few of the many spiritual discernment methods—activities, such as spiritual reading, that people use to become more receptive to God's guidance. If you are interested in learning more about discernment methods, a number of other books describe them. My intent here is to discuss a few principles for using discernment methods to deepen our relationship with God.

If we think a particular discernment method must be used in order to hear God's messages, then we will not be receptive to divine guidance at other times. Discernment methods are most effective when they are an *additional* way to hear God speak. Also, there is no one method that is better than another. Any spiritual practice can be done with the intent to be particularly open to divine will. I believe God guides us to the particular discernment method that will help us to hear more clearly and also that will deepen our divine-human relationship.

Regardless of the methods we use, we deepen our relationships when we consult our Beloved when making decisions.

Relationship-Building Exercise: Timeline of Decisions

1. Draw a timeline from birth to the present. Write a word or phrase at several points on the timeline to indicate five decisions you have made at various times in your life. Choose a variety of decisions—ones that were positive or negative; ones that you are pleased with, embarrassed by, frustrated with, proud of, and so forth. Try to have at least one decision from each stage of your life so far.

2. Focus on each decision in turn, remembering it in as much detail as possible, and answer the following:

   (a) What was happening generally in your life at that time?

   (b) What gifts did you use to make the decision?

   (c) Did you consciously include God in the process?

   (d) Whether or not you consciously included God, are you able to see now how were you offered divine guidance?

   (e) Did the divine guidance provide you with an idea or information that you had not considered?

7

Ride the Rhythms of Relationship

For everything there is a season,
and a time for every matter under heaven. . . .
a time to embrace, and a time to refrain from embracing;
a time to seek, and a time to lose; . . .
a time to keep silence, and a time to speak.
(Ecclesiastes 3:1, 5-7)

s this scripture from Ecclesiastes says, there are times when the two in relationship "embrace" and times when they "refrain from embracing"—times when one or both experience the other as close or distant. One of the most difficult times for many people of faith is when God seems to have left the relationship. Yet the Holy One tells us through many prophets, "I will never leave you or forsake you" (Hebrews 13:5). Why, then, does it sometimes seem that God has deserted us?

There are a number of reasons for God's seeming absence. We will examine some of them, beginning with times when it is we who, wittingly or unwittingly, step away from the relationship.

When We Step Away from God

Are there things about God that frustrate you? Sometimes, I want God to be made in my likeness, rather than the other way around. I want a God who will give me what I want the way I want it, and I get frustrated when my wishes are not met. Sometimes, I turn my back on God and sulk. I continue to try to

51

control God, at times, even though I know that God's way is best.

I believe all of us will have times when we are in conflict with God, even though we are the only ones taking part in the conflict. And, in fact, relationships can be enhanced by friction. It is a well-known principle of group dynamics that times of conflict and their successful resolution are necessary to deepen intimacy and empathy in the interactions. Many people have the experience of increased closeness after they have "fought and made up." I believe the same dynamic takes place in our divine-human relationship. I have talked with many people who are angry at God for not fulfilling some wish in the manner they specified. They withdraw from God, maybe going so far as to say God is dead or uncaring. They do not respond to divine invitations to heal. It is when we bring our frustration and anger to God that we are more likely to see the insights and resolution God is offering.

We also create distance in the divine-human relationship when we have incorrect beliefs about the Holy One. For example, believing that God is for "us" and against "them" has caused many people to kill others in the name of the Prince of Peace. If we are receptive to the Spirit's guidance, though, our incorrect beliefs will undergo refinement—an often uncomfortable yet freeing experience.

Another example of a restrictive belief that distances us from God is thinking of God as a punitive Deity. Over and over again, Jesus invited us to see God as loving, approachable, merciful, forgiving, and just. Yet, some Christians cling to an image of God as a fierce old man who keeps track of all our transgressions and punishes us if we make the slightest mistake.

So, we can feel distant from God through our own actions, such as misunderstandings and restrictive images. And it is natural for each of us to experience conflict in the relationship. Thankfully, the relationship is deepened when we bring these concerns to the refining fire of the Holy Spirit.

When God Is with Us in a New Way

Christians through the ages have spoken of times when God has seemed absent, and it is only later—sometimes years later—that they realize God was stepping differently, not stepping away. Sometimes God comes to us in ways we are unfamiliar with, and we don't recognize the hand of the Holy.

Rose told me that she had gone through a six-month period when she experienced God's guidance as a strong sense of peace almost daily. She grew in her receptivity and gratitude to God. A week previous to our visit, the guidance had stopped, and she was feeling bereft. What had she done wrong? Where was God?

After we had discussed this for some time, I invited Rose to take her concerns to God in prayer. The next time we met, she related that although she still complained periodically about the lack of guidance, she had discovered what God was up to. She explained:

> When I first sat to pray, I was pretty agitated. It took a few prayer sessions before I was calm enough to listen to God. Then I got a sense similar to training wheels coming off a bicycle. "Oh, no," I said to God. "I can't make decisions on my own. I don't trust myself." As clear as anything, I heard a voice within that replied, "Well, I trust you." I still feel tingly inside when I think of it. God trusts me! I know now that the work that needs to be done to deepen my relationship with God is to learn to trust myself more.

So, for Rose, God was stepping differently in her life to help her grow psychologically and spiritually.

How do we recognize God when our Beloved is coming to us in an unfamiliar way? A story from the Gospel of Luke may help answer that question.

It was the first Easter the world had ever known. Yet two people, followers of the man they believed to be the Messiah, were unaware of the wonderful events of that day as they sadly trudged along the road to Emmaus.

Jesus joined them as they walked, though they didn't recognize him. When they shared their despair about what had happened to Jesus of Nazareth in Jerusalem, Jesus responded by interpreting all the scriptures that had foretold the suffering and death of the Messiah before he could "enter into his glory." The two still didn't realize to whom they were speaking. In spite of their feelings of despair, however, they urged Jesus to stay and eat with them, and as he broke the bread they recognized him. At that moment he vanished. They immediately returned to their community in Jerusalem (Luke 24:13-35).

When we are experiencing pain or loss, we tend to protect our vulnerability by withdrawing. Yet these believers on the road to Emmaus, in their pain and sadness, demonstrated hospitality—a core value of God they had accepted for themselves. And I believe that because they were visibly living their faith, they were more receptive to "recognizing" Jesus when he blessed and broke the bread at supper.

When we are highly stressed or in a crisis situation, there is no time to decide how we are going to react. So we behave in familiar ways. If living our beliefs is familiar to us, as it was to the people on the Emmaus road, we will act out of those beliefs during difficult times. And, I believe, we are more likely to see God's presence.

When It Seems That God Steps Away

Saint John of the Cross called it "the dark night of the soul." It is a time of life when it seems as if God has stepped away from us. When the dark night is experienced, persons may feel depressed or anxious, or believe that God is no longer with them.

Yet they continue to live Christian beliefs and values. They continue to seek for God, even though spiritual practices may seem dry and unsatisfying.

Seekers may look back on their dark night many years later and realize the spiritual fruit that matured during this time. Their relationship with God was refined as they grew in qualities such as trust, compassion, and love. In hindsight, they often see God's guiding hand—though it was in ways they couldn't recognize at the time.

The dark night of the soul is complex, and it's beyond the scope of this book to do more than touch on it. If you want more information, I suggest Dr. Gerald May's book *The Dark Night of the Soul: A Psychiatrist Explores the Connection Between Darkness and Spiritual Growth* (HarperCollins, 2005).

If you are experiencing a prolonged period of God's seeming absence, it may be helpful to speak to a spiritual director. These people are experienced at accompanying others on their spiritual journey. They help clarify issues and give support without telling the seeker what to believe. Spiritual Directors International has more than 5,000 members worldwide, and you will be able to find a director in your geographical area at www.sdiworld.org.

When God seems absent or when we feel overwhelmed by our restrictions and attachments, it may bring comfort to remember God's words of commitment to the divine-human relationship: "I have called you by name, you are mine. When you pass through the waters, I will be with you; and through the rivers, they shall not overwhelm you" (Isaiah 43:1-2).

Relationship-Building Exercise: Ebb and Flow

1. Draw a timeline from birth to the present in one color. Mark it off in five-year increments. With another color, draw "waves" of significant positive and negative experiences in your life. Five to eight is a manageable number. You may choose to draw the

positive waves above the timeline and the negative ones below. You may choose to name the waves with a word or short phrase.

2. When you are finished, take each wave in turn and remember that time in detail. What happened? How did it affect you? It might take a number of sessions to complete all your waves. Some people find it helpful to write their answers in a journal or on a piece of paper.

3. Now remember whether you were aware of God's presence at that particular time. With the third color, write "present" or "absent" beside each of the significant experiences. You may wish to list some of the ways God was visible to you—such as feeling comforted during prayer or guided by a sermon—as well as what it was like to experience God as absent—such as feeling confused, angry, or betrayed.

4. In turn, take each of the waves that indicate your experience of God's presence or absence. Give thanks for the times when you felt comforted, guided, or loved by the Holy One. Then focus on each of the times when God seemed absent and hold them up in prayer. Ask to see where God was in your life during this painful time. Be patient, for the answer may come soon or late.

8

Forgive and Accept Forgiveness

One who forgives an affront fosters friendship,
but one who dwells on disputes will alienate a friend.
(Proverbs 17:9)

aleb and Nicole had been coming for relationship counseling for a month, when Caleb dropped a bombshell. He confessed to having an affair, long ago, in the early years of their marriage. Instead of showing the shock I imagine he was expecting, Nicole only nodded sadly and said, "I wasn't aware of the details, but I knew something happened back then. I've been a bit suspicious of you ever since. I've even kept a secret bank account, in case you suddenly dumped me. I had to protect myself."

So, for years the couple has lived together without the deep trust and freedom that could have been theirs. Couples who are aware of wrongs yet ignore them use up a lot of energy "averting their eyes" and "protecting" themselves from future hurts. For relationships to truly grow, wrongs must be acknowledged, worked through, and forgiven.

There is a sphere of influence around each of us. Every word and behavior has some type of impact, not only on those closest to us but also on others—even the world around us. You may have noticed, for example, how an estrangement between two people changes the interactions in their family and friendship circles. This is called a "ripple effect," a term based on the experience of tossing a pebble into a still pond.

Because God is present in our every experience and has concern for all of creation, each of our thoughts, words, and actions has an impact on the divine-human relationship as well. Apologizing to God means being repentant for wrongs directed specifically toward God, as well as wrongs we do to other people and to all of creation—for all wrongs we commit, including those against other people and creation, are wrongs committed against God, who is in all and concerned for all.

Confession, Repentance, and Acceptance

The topic of confession and repentance is a difficult one for many people. Some refuse to acknowledge their sins, even to themselves. For whatever reason, they believe they will be unacceptable to themselves or others or God if they do wrong. Unfortunately, this denial of truth distances them from the author of all truth. (See 1 John 1:8-9.)

Some people confess their transgressions without experiencing remorse. They harbor feelings of defensiveness, resentment, and self-justification. The result is a stepping away from truth and from God. These people are not taking responsibility for their words and actions. Consequently, they will not be able to accept God's grace and mercy.

Other people find it hard to admit wrongs without experiencing crippling shame. They confess, yet their shame and guilt do not allow God's forgiveness to touch them. I have met people who have punished themselves for thirty years or longer because of one wrongdoing. Some of these punishments included never eating dessert, avoiding marriage, refusing to take vacations, and refraining from any enjoyable activity.

These "offenders" thought they were admitting to and atoning for their wrongdoing. They weren't! In fact, they were adding more sin. True atonement, or making amends, is a process of healing for all who have been restricted or bound by the "offense"—and this definitely includes the sinner. Because we are human and have free will, we will continue to sin. With God's help, however, we can become aware more quickly of those times when we are moving into hurtful thoughts, words, or actions. With God's help, we can take responsibility for what we have done, work in partnership with the Spirit for reconciliation, and move toward healing and a more Christlike life.

The Willingness to Forgive

It is natural to be frustrated and angry when we don't get what we want or when the path we want to take seems to be blocked. As Jesus demonstrated in his incarnate life, we can experience these emotions and still forgive the people or things involved in the situation. At times, Jesus showed anger and frustration—at the religious authorities, at his own disciples, at hypocritical people—yet he always forgave them.

Jesus tells us to pray with a forgiving attitude: "Whenever you stand praying, forgive, if you have anything against anyone; so that your Father in heaven may also forgive you your trespasses" (Mark 11:25). Jesus knew that even if the focus of our prayer has nothing to do with the person or situation that we are unwilling to forgive, the "bondage" of a hardened heart will have a negative impact on the connection to God in prayer. It will harm our divine-human relationship.

Refusing to forgive often results in a wary, suspicious, or closed-life pattern. We defend ourselves from imagined future hurts by not letting others touch us deeply. We close ourselves to others. Though we do not experience the pains of relationship, neither do we experience the pleasures. God wants us both to give and accept forgiveness; yet if we are living in a closed pattern, it is difficult to let the healing power of God touch us.

Deepening Our Relationship with God

God is closer to us than our breath and lives even within the closed, hard hearts of unforgivenness and the broken hearts of those who are blamed. God does not reject us when we refuse to forgive. We, on the other hand, reject the call "to do justice, and to love kindness, and to walk humbly with your God" (Micah 6:8). So, we step away from God and God's ways when we do not forgive. We have already seen that the same movement away from our Beloved occurs when we will not confess, repent, or allow forgiveness.

Forgiveness is a gift. It is one that God has given to each of us, yet many people do not know how to unpack and use it. The Holy Spirit is on call twenty-four hours a day to help us with this gift. Many people have told me of the divine guidance they received when they finally called for assistance. Though learning to forgive may take some time, being receptive to the promptings of the Spirit at all times will benefit our divine-human connection. The relationship-building exercise at the end of this chapter was "given" to me when I was having difficulty letting go of resentment and finally asked for the Spirit's help.

One of the most beautiful ways we deepen the divine-human relationship is when we extend forgiveness to others. In those moments we become more like the one who, in the agony of crucifixion, said, "Father, forgive them; for they do not know what they are doing" (Luke 23:34).

Relationship-Building Exercise: Learning to Forgive

1. Spend a few minutes in prayer with the intent to be receptive to God's guidance, particularly about forgiveness.

2. Then, remember a time when you did something wrong and the person you wronged forgave you. The transgression might have been small or large—from recent times or long ago. For this

exercise, the memory needs to include your acceptance of the for-giveness that was offered.

3. Now focus on the internal experience of being forgiven. What words or phrases come to your mind? Write them on the paper. You may think you are finished after writing one or two words; if you are doing this exercise alone, sit a little longer, remembering the experience, and see if any more descriptors emerge. After you finish, let go of that memory and settle your-self prior to shifting your focus.

4. Remember a time when another person wronged you—a small or large offense from the recent or long-ago past—and you forgave that person. The experience needs to be one in which you truly experienced forgiveness in your being. Saying "I forgive you" because "it's the Christian thing to do" or because someone said you should will not work for this exercise. It doesn't matter if the other person accepted your forgiveness; the focus for this part of the exercise is on your experience.

5. As you remember the experience of forgiving another, what words or phrases come to your mind? Write them on the paper. Again, you may think you are finished after writing one or two words; if you are doing this exercise alone, sit a little longer, remembering the experience, and see if any more descriptors emerge.

6. Now, look at the words that describe being forgiven and for-giving. Do you notice a similarity? Both giving and receiving true forgiveness lead to an increase in love and freedom.

9

Share Your Pain
as Well as Your Joy

My heart is stricken and withered like grass;
I am too wasted to eat my bread. (Psalm 102:4)

Josh ran weeping into the room, and threw himself at his mother, who had just handed me a cup of tea. Kate scooped the boy up, holding him close and stroking his head. After a few moments, the tears stopped and the three-year-old asked to be put down. As he ran off, I asked, "What was that about?" "I don't know," Kate replied, "but he just wanted me to acknowledge his feelings and give him comfort and love."

Josh shared his pain with one he loved dearly. Carla, on the other hand, believed it was wrong to do so. She came to me for counseling after a beloved aunt died. Carla decribed her problem as a lack of faith.

"If I had enough faith," she said, "all I would feel was joy that my aunt has gone to her true home."

"Carla," I replied, "if I'm hearing you correctly, you're saying that a strong faith would keep you from grieving, and you're worried that your tears mean your faith is weak."

"That's right," she said. "I try to be as much like Jesus as possible. He wouldn't grieve."

I took my Bible off the bookshelf and had her read what happened just before Jesus raised Lazarus from the dead. She stopped when she came to the verse, "Jesus began to weep" (John 11:35).

"Can you imagine a reason Jesus would be 'greatly disturbed in spirit and deeply moved' in that situation?" I asked her.

Carla thought for a moment, and then smiled. "The only reason I can think of is that Jesus was crying out of compassion for the emotional pain his friends were in." She was silent for a few moments and then continued. "So, Jesus grieved. And his faith was the greatest. I guess that means I can grieve, too."

"Actually," I responded, "I believe God gave us the grieving process to help us heal."

Letting God Heal Us

When we allow ourselves to grieve, we come to understand the many meanings a person, place, job, home, or some other thing held for us. We can be grateful for the connections and learnings we had while the "lost one" was in our life, and we can look to see how God's presence was manifested through that time.

Sharing our pain with God allows us to be more receptive to the healing the Holy One offers us. Some people are hesitant to let God know how they really feel, yet it is only by expressing ourselves truthfully, sharing our anger or despair with God, that we can experience God's healing power. The Bible gives us great suggestions for talking to God in our pain—so many suggestions that I see it as a "grief therapy manual."

For example, various psalms speak of a wide range of concerns and feelings that can help us "cry out" our pain to God, such as Psalm 6:2 "O Lord, heal me!"; Psalm 22:1 "Why have you forsaken me?"; and Psalm 13:1b "How long will you hide your face from me?" Reading them out loud or silently may bring clarity to your own situation, a sense of comfort, or divine guidance.

How God Heals

A few years ago, Mike told the other participants in a workshop that he had been praying for his cancer to be healed, but God wasn't answering his prayers. "I meet with my prayer circle at church every Tuesday," he said, "and the cancer is getting worse. What am I doing wrong?" I invited him to direct that question to God and be receptive to an answer as we continued the workshop.

During the afternoon question period, Mike said, "Well, I'm realizing now that there is a difference between 'healing' and 'cure.' Cure would mean my cancer was completely gone. Sometimes that happens. Healing is being given when I receive what I need to 'live' with the reality of my cancer, not just 'exist' with it."

God heals us by offering, often through other people, the love, forgiveness, strength, mercy, and guidance we need to live meaningfully during times of loss. Even when we think God is far away, there are always traces of God's loving presence if we will look for them. If we don't expect to find God's healing presence in our lives, we can easily overlook divine traces, some of which may be very subtle.

Some people doubt that God would or could help them. As part of my graduate studies, I conducted research with bereaved parents into how their beliefs were affected by their grief. The majority of the grieving parents described a period of doubt about their beliefs at some point in the first year after their loss. Almost all of these "doubters" said that they came through this period with a stronger faith. So, let's look at this issue, since it is easy to feel guilty about doubting God and then to pull away from the relationship.

The Benefits of Doubt

Just after Mary Magdalene reported her experience at the empty tomb, the disciples were gathered behind locked doors for fear of the authorities. Jesus appeared to them, showing his hands and his side.

But Thomas was not with them, and he doubted they had really seen the Lord. When Jesus appeared to them again, Thomas was present. Jesus' response to Thomas's honest doubt was not to rebuke Thomas, but to draw closer and let the disciple touch him (John 20:24-29).

When we express doubt to our Beloved, God will help us with it. If, however, we pull away and close ourselves off from God in our doubt, we may not see the invitation to "touch." God draws closer to us when we are doubting, being present to us in many different ways, until finally we experience the divine presence. Sometimes this realization can take years, especially if we pull away from God in our doubting.

Common doubts during the grieving process include doubt that God is present or wanting to heal us; doubt that we are worthy of being healed; doubt that we are grieving correctly, especially if others tell us we are doing it incorrectly; and doubts that we will ever have a satisfying life again. If we move toward God with these doubts, we will more easily see the divine working through other people, often people we do not expect to be helpful. We may also "touch" God in experiences such as reading scripture and other inspiring texts, observing nature, and doing spiritual practices.

Change Can Bring Healing

Often during the grieving process, the ways we are used to living in relationship to God change. This includes spiritual practices such as prayer and meditation, attending worship services, and reading inspirational texts. As our healing needs change, we may not be able to sustain some of these practices as we used to.

If spiritual practices suddenly feel "dry" and God seems far away, it may be that we are being invited into another way of being with the Divine Healer. Watching and listening for divine "nudges" can help us find the practices we need.

If a different spiritual practice is called for, the Spirit will guide you to it. So, don't assume that just because your spiritual practices seem unsatisfying, they need to be changed. I have talked with many people who spent weeks or months sticking with a practice that didn't give them the sense of comfort or peace or awareness of God's presence for which they longed because they did not have a sense they were being invited to a different practice. Sometime later they were able to look back and see the healing partially brought about by their faithful persistence. For, whether we realize it or not, God is with us.

God does not create our pain and suffering; yet God, whose very essence is love, chooses to be with us in our pain, to feel it and offer us healing.

Relationship-Building Exercise: Clarifying God's Guidance During Difficult Times

Answering the following questions may increase your sensitivity to God's guidance and clarify which spiritual practice is helpful during times of loss and stress.

1. What worries and concerns are currently part of your life right now? What healing do you need?

2. What spiritual practices are appealing to you right now? What attracts you to them?

3. How do you usually experience guidance by the Holy Spirit? How is that happening now?

4. Is the Spirit guiding you in a new way?

10

Take Time Just to Be Together

But now more than ever the word about Jesus spread abroad;
many crowds would gather to hear him and to be cured of their
diseases. But he would withdraw to deserted places and pray.
(Luke 5:15-16)

Tonya and Alison have been close friends for many years. They spend time together every week, sometimes in organized activity, volunteering at a women's shelter, and other times just being together, walking in the park or sharing a meal. Alison told me that the times of just being together—"hanging out"—have deepened their relationship more that the busier, structured ones. During these unstructured times there are often long, comfortable silences between the friends. Sometimes they are moved to share thoughts, feelings, and dreams. There are spaces for laughter and tears, joys and sorrows. A sense of love and gratitude for the other's friendship pervades these special times.

Similarly, when we choose to spend time alone with God, we make a commitment to increased intimacy, to learning more about our Beloved.

The God who cares for us so much—"See, I have inscribed you on the palms of my hand" (Isaiah 49:16)—wants our relationship to be one of love and freedom. We have been given free will, so we do not *need* to develop an intimate relationship with our Maker. We will be loved unconditionally, even if we do not consider God in our daily lives. But what an impoverished existence that would be! We can turn from God to the world in an attempt to meet our needs. Or we can spend time with the One from whom all gifts have originated. Yet, for many Christians, just "hanging out" with God is an unfamiliar experience.

What type of prayer "calls" do you make? For some folks, their most frequent communications with God are emergency 911 calls: "Help, God, I need rescuing!" Others tend to make directory assistance calls: "Please guide me, God." And some make person-to-person calls just for the sake of being together. During this type of call, problems and concerns might be shared, but the main purpose is simply to "connect," to be with the One you love.

There is nothing wrong with the first two types of prayers; our God longs to be of assistance to us. It is the third type of prayer, however, repeated many times throughout a lifetime, that helps us develop the unique, intimate relationship God offers each one of us.

A Personal God

As we get to know people, we have more words to describe their nature, interests, likes, and dislikes. As I passed by two women speaking of a third person at a party, I heard one of them say, "We go line-dancing together every Monday evening. She's so quick at picking up the new steps." Just before I moved out of earshot, one of them mentioned a name. I was surprised. They're talking about a close friend of mine, I thought to myself, except when I describe her, I don't usually mention line-dancing. Even though I know she loves it, that's not a part of our relationship.

Similarly, each of us has a unique relationship with God. We have favorite images of our Beloved. No one image, no matter how rich, can encompass our infinite Creator. In fact, the more images or descriptors of God that resonate with us, the fuller our relationship will be. Each way of thinking about and connecting with God will have a different emotional and spiritual "flavor." For example, we respond somewhat differently to God when we view our relationship as a parent-child relationship than we do when we think of it as an intimate relationship between two lovers.

What are your favorite images of God? Here are a few to consider:

God, Creator—Father, Mother, Source of Being, Holy Mystery, Rock of Ages, Shepherd, King, Lord, Eternal One

Jesus Christ—Eternal Word, Lamb of God, Morning Star, Friend, Teacher, Leader, Son of God, Messiah, Human One, Savior, Redeemer

Holy Spirit—Advocate, Comforter, Breath of God, Fire from Heaven, Spirit of Life, Wisdom Sophia, Consoler, Sustainer

Each of these images reflects a different experience of God. So, having a variety of images for our Beloved will help us to "recognize" more of the ways God may come to us. I frequently ask God, "How do you want me to experience you right now?" I am often surprised by the "answers."

Daily Time with God

An important way we deepen the divine-human relationship is by spending part of each day with our Beloved. It is the norm today for many people to be overbooked—too little time and too many things to be done in that time. I frequently hear couples say they want to deepen their relationship, yet they hardly ever see each other.

It can be the same in our relationship with God. If it is difficult to find time to be alone with God, you may need to change the word "find" to "make." When something is a priority, we "make" time for it. It is not enough to hope the space will come.

Many people are helped by blocking off time on their daily calendar for "dates" with God. Early morning prayer may draw you. Or another time of day may be just right for you to drink more deeply at the Well. Every person and every relationship has its own rhythms. I often find that a prayer time right after lunch refreshes me and focuses me more fully on the One who has been supporting and guiding me all morning. You may try a number of different times to be alone with God until you are ready to choose the one that fits best.

Once you make the time, what should you do and how long should you do it? Ask God to guide you. The Spirit often puts a desire in our hearts for a certain type of spiritual practice. I love to put on a CD of my favorite Christian singers and sing love and gratitude songs to God. A friend of mine said, "When I first heard about Christian meditation, developed by John Main, I just knew this was the practice for me." Do not hold on too tightly to a favorite spiritual practice, though. Stay receptive to the Spirit, who will help you find new ways, as needed, of being in the divine-human relationship.

Also, ask God about the right length of time for your daily spiritual practice. Remember, quality is more important than quantity. It does take us some time to turn our focus from the world to our Beloved, so a prayer period of two or three minutes will probably be no more than a quick, "Hi, God." For many people, twenty minutes once or twice a day seems right. I know one man who says that spending ten minutes in prayer a number of times a day benefits his relationship with God; and I know a woman who needs a longer focusing time, so her prayer time is half an hour.

No matter what your scheduled daily prayer time is like, hold the intent to be receptive to the Divine Presence at all times. There will be many opportunities for God to touch you and for you to touch God throughout the day. You also may discover that sometimes during your daily time with God, a longing may come for a more extended time with God.

Longing for More

At times, we may need a more extended time alone with God, just as the first disciples did. In Mark we read that Jesus sent out his apostles to heal and teach, guided by the Spirit. Even though they were receptive to God every day, as Jesus had taught them, he said when they returned, "Come away to a deserted place all by yourselves and rest a while" (Mark 6:30-31). Although full of the excitement of their successful ministry, the apostles were tired, and Jesus knew they needed a retreat time.

If you wish for more time with God, there are many ways to do so. One option is going to a retreat center for a weekend or longer. To find a retreat center near you, check with your church, denominational Web site, or Retreats International (www.retreatsintl.org). A friend of mine takes a retreat day at home a couple of times a year to focus on God. As she is nudged by the Spirit, she may go for a walk, or to an art gallery, or out to lunch. All activity is done with the consciousness that she and God are "hanging out." Some people spend extended times with God by undertaking pilgrimages, walking to a specific place associated with God. The pilgrimage may range from a day to weeks or months.

When we spend time alone with God, we will experience more divine self-revelation. The relationship with our Beloved will become broader and deeper, and we will understand the delight of the psalmist who said:

> How lovely is your dwelling place,
>   O LORD of hosts!
> My soul longs, indeed it faints
>   for the courts of the Lord;

> my heart and my flesh sing for joy
>> to the living God. . . .
> For a day in your courts is better
>> than a thousand elsewhere. (Psalm 84:1, 10a)

Relationship-Building Exercise: Images of God

1. Remember one of the images of God you had as a child. Draw the image if you find that helpful. Then ask yourself any of the following questions that seem relevant:

- Where did the image come from—another person? scripture? a personal experience?
- How did the image influence your relationship with God—positively and negatively?
- Has the image changed over the years? How did that happen?
- Which person of the Holy Trinity does the image relate to most closely? Did you have images for the other two Persons? What were they?

2. Choose one image of God that speaks to you now. Draw it if you wish.

- How did this image come to be?
- How does it influence your relationship with God—positively and negatively?
- Which Person of the Holy Trinity does the image relate to most closely? Do you have images for the other two Persons? What are they?

11

Don't Be Afraid
to Show Your True Self

One who gives an honest answer
gives a kiss on the lips. (Proverbs 24:26)

We've all had experiences with other persons who have acted in a deceitful manner and, as a result, have seen how destructive dishonesty can be to a relationship. When people act dishonestly, they are hiding their true selves from others. Although many folks would never set out to deceive others in order to harm them, they frequently practice another form of dishonesty. I saw an example of this recently at a congregational workshop.

We were talking about the importance of showing our true selves. Roy said, "I definitely hide certain parts of myself from others. I'm not really being dishonest. I just try to represent myself in the best possible light. It's not hurting anyone." One of the other participants, responded, "Actually, Roy, I've liked you for years, but I don't really know you. I have the sense you're putting on a false front. I don't know how far I can trust you."

Roy was quiet for some time after that. At lunch break, I saw the two friends eating together and deep in conversation. That afternoon, Roy reopened the topic, "I'm realizing how hurtful pretense can be to a relationship. I'm not sure about God, though. God knows me better that I know myself. How can it

75

hurt our relationship if I present myself as somewhat better than I am?"

I answered, "I believe God's great heart sorrows anytime we deny who we really are. When we get 'dressed up for God' we are not bringing our true selves to the relationship."

In the parable of the sower, Jesus speaks of seed falling on several surfaces. Only the seed which landed on good soil produced healthy plants. He explained this parable by saying that the seed is the word of God. God's word flourishes in those who hear it and "hold it fast in an honest and good heart " (Luke 8:11-15).

It is interesting that of all the adjectives Jesus could have used to describe the person who walks in God's ways, he chose "honest" and "good." Lies are illusions. Lying or behaving in an untruthful manner means living in illusion. Since God is the ultimate reality, the act of lying turns us away from the true divine-human relationship.

God, however, can see through all of our deceits and knows that our dishonesty often comes from anxiety, low self-esteem, or other emotional woundedness. God forgives us and loves us unconditionally, and yet God will not coerce us back into honesty and truth. Because we have free will, we need to use that will to accept God's forgiveness and love, and embrace honesty and truth.

Taking Responsibility

Whenever Jesus heard people speaking honestly, he knew that the truth of his teaching would fall on "good soil." The Samaritan woman at the well asked Jesus for the water of eternal life. He tested her honesty, and when he saw she was willing to take responsibility for her actions, he gave her what she asked for (John 4:16-18).

He then went on to teach her, speaking of the differences

between the Samaritan and Jewish faith traditions. Then he said, "But the hour is coming, and is now here, when the true worshipers will worship the Father in spirit and truth, for the Father seeks such as these to worship him. God is spirit, and those who worship him must worship in spirit and truth" (John 4:23-24).

The Samaritan woman took responsibility for her actions, even though many would judge her for them. I imagine it was a surprise when Jesus praised her for her honesty and honored her by speaking deep, spiritual truths.

Jesus tells us true worship is done in "spirit and truth." One meaning of worshiping in truth is to be "honest to God"—to bring ourselves to God in a genuine manner, showing ourselves as we truly are with our weaknesses, sins, and doubts as well as our gifts, virtues, and strengths.

Acknowledging our pain, weaknesses, and faults makes it easier to accept God's invitation to transformation and healing. When Jesus was angry, sad, frustrated, or fearful, it was very visible. He was honest in his feelings and issues with people and with God. In the garden of Gethsemane, he told his disciples, "I am deeply grieved, even to death," and he prayed, "Abba, Father, for you all things are possible; remove this cup from me; yet, not what I want, but what you want" (Mark 14:34, 36).

Jesus took responsibility for his feelings, and was not afraid to share his experience honestly with Abba and with his followers. Honesty and responsibility go together. I believe it is not possible to have one without the other. By cultivating these two qualities, we become more Christlike. Jesus lived in an authentic way and encouraged us to do the same.

Authentic Living

To live in a fully honest manner, then, is to do more than tell the truth. Honest living is authentic living—taking

responsibility for one's thoughts and actions, having a clear purpose, living a deep meaning, and being emotionally suitable for
the circumstances. In order to live an authentic life, we must take
ourselves off "autopilot" and stop reacting to situations in familiar
ways without thinking—or in ways that family or society say are
right. We must hold the intent to see through to the truth of every
situation. And in the truth of every situation, we will find God.

Living an authentic life in relationship with God is essentially
being transparent to our Beloved. And when our reality meets
the infinite Reality, whatever needs to change in us will be
refined in the furnace of God's love. Over time, we will grow into
the free, loving people God longs for us to be. And we will live
in greater intimacy with our Beloved, because, as it says in the
proverb, "One who gives an honest answer gives a kiss on the
lips" (Proverbs 24:26).

Relationship-Building Exercise:
Examen (or Examination) of Conscience

The spiritual practice *examen of conscience* is much older than
Christianity. God has spoken into the hearts and minds of people
of all faiths and ages, stirring them to look at their thoughts and
actions in light of divine law. Many Christians include an exam-
en of conscience as a daily evening practice. Some conduct the
examen two or three times a day for a period of several weeks, or
even longer, when they have the sense that God is inviting them
to allow transformation of a specific restrictive attitude or behavior pattern. Honesty with self and God is a prerequisite for this
spiritual practice.

General Examen (to be done in the evening)

This is a general overview of your thoughts and actions from
the day just past. Move into prayer and examine your behaviors

and thoughts in the context of divine law. As you slowly remember the day, focus on both positive and negative thoughts and actions. You may wish to structure the examen in the following manner:

1. What God-given blessings are you thankful for? Some blessings may be obvious; others take more reflection. You may find that journaling brings the memories into sharper relief. When you have given thanks to God for all your blessings, move to the next question.

2. When have your thoughts or actions been counter to God's grace and divine law? If this is difficult to answer, it may help to look closely at thoughts and actions that seem comfortable or familiar. Ask God's forgiveness for each restriction you find. Don't rush this process. "Listen" attentively to God's response to your confession. Let the realization sink in that you are forgiven. Let God know you are receptive to transformation of your restrictive patterns.

3. Now focus on tomorrow. Think about the day that is planned with the intent to uncover situations that may be challenging and, therefore, may trigger your restrictive patterns. Express the intent to follow God's guidance. Use your God-given gifts, in the presence of the Holy Spirit, to discern how to meet tomorrow's challenges. Psychological research shows that if people rehearse future situations, they are more likely to act in the way they have practiced. This has even more impact if you make the rehearsal as real as possible, such as speaking aloud the words you wish to use.

12

Listen to Your Loved One

*Your words were found, and I ate them,
and your words became to me a joy
and the delight of my heart. (Jeremiah 15:16)*

Jacques had a stroke three years ago. He communicates slowly, using eye blinks and cards, with everyone but Anna, his wife of forty-five years. Anna, unlike the others, usually knows what Jacques is thinking or wants to say. When I asked how she became so skilled at understanding Jacques, she smiled and replied, "I've listened to him a lot over the years. Still, it's important that I don't assume what he wants. So, I still check out that I've heard correctly."

Being Fully Attentive

How much work does God have to do to get our attention? When our Creator tells us something, offers us an insight to help us on our path through life, or simply says, "I love you," how often is the message drowned out by our distractions? What percentage of our prayer time is spent in talking to God and what percentage in listening to God? What does it mean to listen to God?

Healthy, intimate relationships give each partner space to talk and to listen. Listening deeply to another is hard work. It asks us to be fully attentive. It cannot be done if we run off to answer the phone as the other is speaking, or if our mind is planning what we will say when the other stops talking. Sometimes deep listening comes naturally. Most often, though, it must be a conscious intention, which takes practice.

One of the aspects of the divine-human relationship is that God frequently seems to be silent. This does not mean, however, that our Beloved is not present or is not communicating with us. Have you ever sat on a park bench in companionable silence with a longtime friend? That silence is full of presence and communication. Not a word has to be spoken. Listening is not done solely with the ears. We learn much more fully about another when we are attentive with all of our senses.

Some people hear God speak in words or phrases that are different from the way they usually speak or think. The communication may be like a cross between a thought and a voice. Many others receive God's communication in different ways, including a sense of peace or rightness; a physical sensation, such as a flow of energy; an emotion, such as unconditional love; a "stirring" in the heart or mind; or the awareness of a Presence. Since we do not know how God will communicate with us, keeping all of our senses attuned to the divine helps us to "hear." The first step in attuning our senses to God is holding the belief that God wants to communicate with us and may choose any moment to do so.

When we cultivate a listening attitude in our relationship with God, we are more likely to recognize those companionable silences when our Beloved's love, acceptance, and pleasure in us is evident. Often this involves patience and receptivity.

Being Patient and Receptive

Rebecca woke one Sunday morning feeling joyous. The previous day she had received word that her mother's surgery was successful and that a close friend had announced her engagement. *I can't wait to get to church and thank God,* she thought. Rebecca told me later that she prepared breakfast and ate it on "auto-pilot." She was focused in happy anticipation on the upcoming church service.

Rebecca took her dishes to the sink and suddenly realized she was not aware of her current reality. Shifting her attention away from her anticipation of the church service, she tuned in to the present moment. She became aware of a bird singing outside her window and a new bloom on her African violet. *Ah, I would have missed this if I were still in the future,* thought Rebecca. *Thank you, God, for this beautiful world.* As Rebecca expanded her awareness to include God, she had a sense that her Creator was enjoying the experience with her. *I'm looking forward to going to church to celebrate your gift of the Holy Spirit to us,* she prayed silently. A knowing came into her heart in response: *I'm no more present there than here.*

What a delightful "God touch" Rebecca had. And she gained the understanding that we don't have to wait for a special time or place to be in communication with our Beloved. When she tuned in to her present reality, Rebecca was also practicing another quality that helps us be fully attentive: receptivity.

To be receptive is to be willing to receive something; including gifts, new ideas, suggestions, and confidences. Being receptive to God means living with the intention to deepen the divine-human relationship. Receptivity must be mixed with love, though, if we are to experience the reality of God. Receptivity without love tends to be exclusive.

Receptivity with love is radically inclusive. It is lived when we know that God is present in all things, at all times, and that everything is God's beloved creation. We can cultivate this loving receptivity by bringing these truths to our awareness a number of times a day. Then, we will realize that every experience we have is an experience shared with our Beloved.

Surrendering Helps Us Listen Attentively to God

Another quality associated with being fully attentive to God is called "spiritual surrender," which is giving back to God that which is God's. We are God's works of art and gifts of love. Spiritual surrender returns the gift to the Giver. Gift and giver become one. The way to do this is simple, yet it can be done only with the grace of God.

Paul says, "I have been crucified with Christ; and it is no longer I who live, but it is Christ who lives in me" (Galatians 2:19-20). When we surrender ourselves to God, we give free rein to the Holy Spirit to refine us. As we become more Christlike, we also become more ourselves. We don't lose our uniqueness. We lose or loosen any attitudes, feelings, thoughts, and behaviors that have kept us bound. When we surrender ourselves to God, the gift is given back better than ever.

Spiritual surrender can become more concrete and, therefore, seem more doable if we think of it in terms of an image or symbol. My own image of surrender is an experience I have with my little dog, Smokey. Lying on the carpet, she seems to be sleeping soundly. Yet she is instantly on her feet and alert if someone enters the room—unless that someone is me.

Although Smokey was supposed to be my daughter's dog, she visibly gave her heart to me when she was only ten weeks old. So, when I enter the room in which she is sleeping, Smokey doesn't move a muscle. When I am close enough to touch her, however, she rolls on her back, showing me her tummy and throat. Her eyes stay closed. It is a position of total surrender. I want to be like that with God.

In prayer, I frequently bring that image of Smokey to mind and "give" myself to God. Also, when I sense the divine presence or feel a "God touch," I am sometimes able to surrender in that moment. Some people find that certain physical positions in prayer encourage surrender, such as bowing or lying prostrate or face up.

Whatever helps you surrender to God must also involve a deep listening. We are not able to "let go into God" if we are focusing on ourselves. Talking keeps our attention on our own needs and desires. Surrender occurs when our total focus is God. All spiritual practices help us deepen the divine-human relationship. And when we have the desire to surrender, God can use any practice to accept the gift of ourselves. As I have said before, I believe we are invited by the Spirit to the spiritual practice that will be best for us at any one time. No one practice is inherently superior to another. There is one, though, called contemplative prayer or meditation, that is particularly associated with spiritual surrender.

Contemplation is not concerned with defining, describing, analyzing. It is about looking at, being present to. We experience oneness with whatever we contemplate, whether a flower or God. Words associated with contemplative prayer include vulnerability, transparency, yielding, and abandonment. It is prayer without words, a "resting in the Lord." It is not done with the expectation of benefit—receiving rest, guidance, or love. It is giving ourselves as a gift for God's own use. In contemplative prayer, the Beloved is our sole focus. People who are called to contemplative prayer may have a designated time of day for this practice. Contemplation can be also practiced as we go about our daily lives if we have interior stillness.

Regardless of the method used to achieve it, spiritual surrender can bring up major trust issues for many people. God understands this and desires, but doesn't demand, this level of intimacy. The Holy Spirit helps us build trust slowly. We just discussed receptivity with love. Well, it's just as important to have trust with love. Trust without love is blind. We may have been in abusive or disrespectful human relationships in which we were told to trust blindly. God does not ask this of us. All that God does and wants us to do incorporates love.

Trust with love is intelligent. It asks questions, as Mary did when the Archangel Gabriel appeared to tell her she would be the mother of God. Mary's response was "How can this be since I am a virgin?" (Luke 1:34). God does not want us to trust blindly. Although we may not receive clear answers to all our questions, our Beloved wants us to ask.

If trusting God is difficult for you, bring that concern to prayer. With the Spirit's help, you may begin to understand in a new way some past experiences—times when you thought God was untrustworthy. The Spirit will help you build trust step by step until you feel safe to surrender spiritually into this awesome Love.

Be Still and Know That I Am God

This well-beloved message from our Creator—"Be still, and know that I am God" (Psalm 46:10)—invites us to listen attentively so that we can grow in awareness and understanding of our Beloved. It is easier to listen fully to another when we are still inside. Patience, receptivity, and spiritual surrender can help us maintain this stillness. Then we will hear divine self-revelation and will know God in the way our Beloved wants to be known. We will say with Jeremiah, "Your words were found, and I ate them, / and your words became to me a joy / and the delight of my heart" (15:16). And we will give thanks for this match made in heaven.

Relationship-Building Exercise: Attentive Listening

1. Remember one example of each of the following and write about/discuss it:

- companionable silence with another person
- companionable silence in nature
- companionable silence with God

2. What is your image of spiritual surrender? Draw or write it. Find a way to keep your image visible in your daily life to remind you to surrender to God.

STUDY GUIDE

Using This Guide

This study guide is based on a format of twelve forty-five-minute sessions intended to be used as a short-term study for a Sunday school class or other small group. Suggestions for other formats, such as a day-long workshop, weekend retreat, or week-long summer camp, can be found on the Web site www.nancyreeves.com.

The material in this study guide is suitable for adults and older youth. It is expected that participants will have read the related chapter prior to the session, as the following discussion questions presume understanding of the concepts.

Forming a Group

You will need at least one person to advertise, organize, and coordinate the study group. This person also may serve as the group facilitator. The facilitator should be present at each group session to welcome members, keep time, and help the members stay on track.

It will help the feeling of safety and trust to have some group rules that are agreeable to all. During the first session, decide which rules the group wishes to use. Write them on a flip chart and post them each week as a reminder. Here are some suggested group rules:

- The group will begin and end on time.
- Share briefly. Everyone deserves to have time to speak.
- Each person chooses his or her level of participation. Silence is fine. No one is to be pressured to share.
- Confidentiality: Everything shared in the group stays in the group.

- Anonymity: Members' identities are not to be shared outside the group.
- No advice-giving. Don't tell others what they should or should not do to deepen their relationship with God.
- This is an educational group intended to discuss spiritual and psychological material. It is not a counseling or psychotherapy group.
- No judgments. All group members are entitled to their own opinions.

Tips for the Facilitator

Many people have never shared details of their spiritual life, and it may feel intimidating for them to do so in a group. Reassure participants by explaining the primary benefit of this kind of sharing, which is that group members may become "spiritual friends" who support, encourage, and guide one another as they deepen their faith. Watch, though, that members do not share too intimately. Some people may get caught up in the accepting atmosphere of the group and later regret that they shared so deeply. If someone begins a story that seems unusually personal, you may want to gently stop them.

You are a member of the group as well. Keep in mind, however, that some members will give your comments more weight because they see you as being in charge. So, after sharing your own stories and thoughts, bring the focus back to the other members by saying something such as, "Now, does anyone else have something they want to say?" Otherwise, members may begin looking to you always to lead the discussion.

Although there may be many diverse ideas in the group, you will need to stop any words that are racist, sexist, slandering, blaming, shaming, or unnecessarily negative. It is easier to do this if you have established a group rule specifying that all group members are entitled to their own opinions and that judgmental comments are not welcome.

Session Outline

Note: The time guidelines shown are estimates only. Feel free to adjust as necessary within the agreed-upon time limit of your group.

Opening Prayer (1-3 minutes)
Ask someone in the group to offer a short opening prayer based on the scripture at the beginning of the chapter.

Chapter Review (3-4 minutes)
The group facilitator may share a very brief synopsis of the chapter to refresh members' memories.

Group Discussion (35 minutes)
Try to discuss at least three of the questions provided for each chapter, being sure to invite a range of responses about different aspects of each topic. Even if only one participant has completed the relationship-building exercise, it may be helpful to include one of the questions on those exercises as well. Remind participants that doing the exercises helps them to integrate the material and clarify aspects of their divine-human relationship.

Responsive Reading (1-3 minutes)
End with a prayer that uses some of the concepts presented in the chapter. (You may want to prepare this prayer in advance of the session.)

Discussion Questions

Chapter 1. Say "I Love You" Frequently

1. When and how have you experienced God's love (physically, mentally, emotionally, spiritually)?

2. What does the following scripture passage mean to you? *The fear of the* LORD *is the beginning of wisdom; / all those who practice it have a good understanding (Psalm 111:10).*

3. What are some of the ways you show your love to God?

From Relationship-Building Exercise
4. What divine attribute do you love most? How do you experience this attribute in your life?

5. What is a favorite scripture selection or hymn that speaks to you of God's love, and why?

Chapter 2. Say and Show Gratitude

1. Have you received an unexpected benefit when you expressed or showed gratitude to another person or to God? If so, tell about it.

2. When have you felt a great need to say thank you to God?

3. What is your favorite way to say thank you to God?

From Relationship-Building Exercise
4. What gift did you choose for this exercise, and how has that gift changed over the years?

5. Give one example of how the Spirit has guided you to use that gift.

6. How are you currently using that gift in your life?

Chapter 3. Give Care and Attention to the Relationship

1. How have you grown in your understanding and experience of God by giving your divine-human relationship care and attention?

2. What are some of your current spiritual practices, and what do they do for your relationship with God?

3. What does the Eucharist, or Holy Communion, mean to you?

4. The Lord's Prayer contains this request: "Give us this day our daily bread." What does "daily bread" mean to you?

From Relationship-Building Exercise
5. What is your favorite day or season of the Christian year, and what are some of the meanings it holds for you?

6. As you completed the exercise, did you discover a time in the Christian year that was unfamiliar to you? What was it, and how might it help you to deepen your relationship with God?

Chapter 4. Develop Self-Awareness to Help the Relationship

1. Describe a moment of self-awareness you were led to by the Holy Spirit sometime in your past.

2. What messages from family, church, or society did you receive about self-love as you were growing up?

3. How has God shown you one of your "weeds" and provided refining or healing for it?

From Relationship-Building Exercise
4. Name one of your qualities, and tell how it has deepened your relationship with God.

Chapter 5. Tell Your Loved One What You Need

1. C. S. Lewis said that we have a strong longing for God that begins in childhood, though often it is misunderstood. Did you have a longing or yearning when you were a child? What did you think that longing was about?

2. What were you taught as a child about bringing your needs to God? Were you taught a spiritual practice to do this?

From Relationship-Building Exercise
3. Describe a time when God's guidance showed you that you were not really aware of your true need.

4. How do you know when you are attached to something or someone in an unhealthy way? For example, do you experience it somewhere in your body (such as a knot in the stomach, sweaty palms, clinched fists)?

5. How do you experience spiritual detachment? Give an example.

Chapter 6. Consult with Each Other When Making Decisions

1. Have you ever tried a spiritual discernment method? What was it, and what was the outcome?

2. Describe times when you have experienced God's messages in or through any of the following: dreams, Scripture, other read-

ings, sermons or homilies, other people, a sense of rightness or deep peace, a physical sensation?

3. What might be some of the reasons Eli ignored God's warnings?

From Relationship-Building Exercise
4. Describe a time you felt divine guidance when making a decision.

5. How do you usually "hear" God's messages?

Chapter 7. Ride the Rhythms of Relationship

1. What was a belief you once held about God or Christianity, perhaps as a child, that later you realized was incorrect and was restricting you or your divine-human relationship?

2. How has the Holy Spirit guided you to awareness of restrictive beliefs (for example, through scripture)?

3. Have you ever experienced a sudden difference in the way God related to you? If so, what was that like for you?

4. Jesus said, "Blessed are you who are poor, for yours is the kingdom of God." What does this statement mean to you?

From Relationship-Building Exercise
5. Have there been many times when God has seemed absent in your life? Tell about one of these times.

6. What has helped you when God seemed absent?

7. Were you able to see God's presence later? How?

Chapter 8. Forgive and Accept Forgiveness

1. What were you taught about forgiveness as a child?

2. Describe your feelings when you have confessed a sin to God and have experienced forgiveness. Do not say what the sin was, unless you feel very comfortable sharing that.

From Relationship-Building Exercise
3. What is it like to be truly forgiven? Do you experience this as a physical sensation? an emotion? some other way?

4. What is it like truly to forgive? Do you experience this as a physical sensation? an emotion? some other way?

Chapter 9. Share Your Pain as Well as Your Joy

1. Have you ever experienced God "weeping" with you? If so, what was that like?

2. Have you ever experienced the difference between curing and healing in your own life? If so, explain.

3. Has a Scripture passage ever comforted or guided you during a time of high stress or grief? If so, describe.

From Relationship-Building Exercise
4. What did you get out of the exercise of sharing your pain with God?

Chapter 10. Take Time Just to Be Together

1. Are you "drawn" to a particular time of day to spend with God? If so, when is it, and why do you think you prefer this time?

2. Is there a particular spiritual practice you are drawn to at this time in your life? If so, what is it, and what do you like about it?

3. Have you ever gone on retreat? If so, what was it like?

4. Describe what the following phrase means to you: "I have carved you on the palm of my hand."

From Relationship-Building Exercise

5. Did you have an image of God as a child? If so, what was it, and where did it come from? How did this image affect your faith and your relationship with God?

6. Is there an image of God that particularly deepens your divine-human relationship at the present time? If so, what is it, and how does it affect your connection with God?

7. Is there one person of the Holy Trinity you tend to pray to more often? If so, do you have any ideas why?

Chapter 11. Don't Be Afraid to Show Your True Self

1. We all have been hypocritical at one time or another in life. How has God shown you a particular hypocrisy in your own life and helped you to let it go?

2. What does it mean for you to "worship in spirit and truth"?

3. Describe a time when you decided to be honest in your relationship with God even though it was difficult.

4. Why do you imagine Jesus wanted his disciples to remain awake in the garden of Gethsemane? What difference would it make if they were awake or asleep?

Study Guide

From Relationship-Building Exercise

5. What was it like to do the examination of conscience? Have you ever done anything like that in the past?

6. Did you learn anything from the practice?

Chapter 12. Listen to Your Loved One

1. Have you had an experience when God drew your attention to a new meaning from familiar Scripture? If so, please describe the insight.

2. How easy or difficult is it for you to have "patience with love"? Has God helped you to be more patient? If so, please describe.

3. Have you "met" God somewhere you least expected? If so, please describe.

4. How have you had the experience that Paul described of being "in Christ"? ("So if anyone is in Christ, there is a new creation: everything old has passed away; see, everything has become new!" [2 Corinthians 5:17])

From Relationship-Building Exercise

5. Describe a time when you experienced companionable silence with God. It could have been a time when you were consciously attentive to God, or a time when you were silent within yourself and became aware of God's silent presence.

6. What is your image of spiritual surrender?

7. Has there been any change in your relationship with God since reading this chapter?